THE
WARFARE

Adegboye Samuel

TABLE OF CONTENTS

Preface

The presence you carry matters in the quest of life. The move of the spirit cannot be ruled out in the battle we face daily. Human being encounters a lot of unseen battles that is unexplainable. The wicked one – the adversary won't stop his haunt until he pulls a destiny out of it canopy. Understanding who you are, and equipping yourself in a realm unseen is mostly important in the race of existence.

One of my most fabulous imagination is how powers are exercised in different territories in this world. Human manifest invincibly in ways beyond natural – taking various forms of creatures for the manifestation of their abilities. The most significant presence that is needed in the supernatural, and in human nature is his *Spirit* — the divine breath which permeates and animates all things. It manifests throughout creation in different kingdoms or degrees.

As there are terestial manifestation of power, the marine spirit are not relaxed to breath out their powers. A lot of people wonder why water spirits are so powerful. Of a truth, I tell you the curious power of destructions and fascinations exercised by water spirits lie in the fact that they belong to one element, and the degree of their effect can be seen in the way the sea displays its anger. To reveal the action of the strength marine spirits, Herbet Saffir and Robert Simpson came up with a scale – saffir simpson scale to physically comprehend the action of hurricane. Herbert saffir was a structural engineer. In 1960, he came up with an observation base on multiple North Atlantic Basin hurricanes, to quantify the extreme damage from the hurricane wind. In 1970s, Robert Simpson expanded the scale by rating the strength and damage made by hurricane from category 1 through category 5. Human knowledge can only compare for comprehension but can never comprehend the manifestation of spiritual powers. This is because they are not from the natural ends, they are from the supernatural ends. However, as human beings, we are the embodiment of the four elements of nature. Marine spirits are so powerful and destructive to human beings because they stimulate the water element within us. Water spirit brings forth in abundance the vitality from the water kingdom, and the energy from the water kingdom energizes the water elements in human. If creatures like us enter into the territory or a relationship with one-element nature like water spirit, we will be poisoned by an overdose of the element (water) which we find ourselves. In the same instance, if any marine spirit comes to exist among us, they suffer a great deal. Do you know why? A single element creature like marine spirit must learn to control and incorporate an additional three elements which becomes a problem.

Of a truth, I tell you that personalities existing in their dark nature lives amongst us, and they are clothed in a human body. Some of them are living with fellow human beings as either husband or wife. Any relationship or mating between human and marine spirit is a hopeless proposition. They present themselves in the human garment they are wearing to mislead us to think they are like us. You might have heard stories of persons in our midst that are marine spirits, for some days they remain in the river and later resurface on planet earth and continue to live with us. Some humans are brought from their previous existences and they possess a natural ability to access the world unseen. These breeds of people are not dark spirits clothed in a perishable human body; instead, they were born with an innate ability to get in touch with the supernatural.

About seventy-one percent of the earth is covered with water, therefore their influence cannot be less emphasized. Spirits in the sea love to associate with human beings. They might start coming to dwell among us taking form of human body. Marine spirits will stimulate the water element in a musician, and this will bring about inspiration and enhancement of the influential power of the musician. The alliance of this spirit is a potent tonic for a musician. However, an average citizen will never benefit from water spirit alliance – that is, an ordinary person who focuses on having a family, wife, children, education, achieve this or achieve that in organized society will be very upset with a water spirit contact. If you examine culture, you will observe that the average individuals are in troubled of darkness invasion alliance.

Dark Aura is a storyline that may help a Christian see the necessity of putting on the whole armour of God to overcome the invasion from the devil's agent – Marine spirit, and to be immovable in that no matter what comes from dark ends, we believe in the saving grace of our Lord Jesus Christ, to deliver us from the snare of fowlers. However, you don't treat spiritual things carnally, but you tackle them spiritually, understanding that,

"For we are not fighting against flesh and blood enemies, but against evil rulers and authorities of the unseen world, against mighty powers in this dark world, and against evil spirits in the heavenly places." Ephesians 6:12 Nlt

In spite that we wrestle not against flesh and blood, the reality of this scripture must be clear that,

"and what is the exceeding greatness of His power toward us who believe, according to the working of His mighty power which He worked in Christ when He raised Him from the dead and seated Him at His right hand in the heavenly places, far above all principality and power and might and dominion, and every name that is named, not only in this age but also in that which is to come. And He put all things under His feet, and

*gave **Him** to be **head** over **all things** to the church, **Ephesian 1:19 – 22 (NKJV).***

It is highly expedient for us *to be of sober spirit, be on the alert. Your adversary, the devil, prowls around like a roaring lion, seeking someone to devour. But resist him. Firm in your faith, knowing that the same experiences of suffering are being accomplished by your brethren who are in the world. After you have suffered a little while, the God of all grace, will himself perfect. Confirm, strengthen and established you – **1peter 5:8-10.***

Chapter 1
The Making

The noise was overwhelming; Michelle couldn't stand the horrible effect of different sounds in her ears. Two agents gripped her hands, each on her side as she tries to break off. Michelle struggled with them, shouting, let me go! Let me go! But the two weird creatures held her tight to walk her to her throne. The congregation of the marine agents and mermaids stood up to welcome the number 2 Queen of the marine spirits. Her seat has been vacant for a long time. No one had been capable of taking the position. No one is as powerful as Michelle. She is the long-awaited Queen. The celebration continues as Michelle struggles to break out. Michelle was finally taken to her seat. As she was about to be forced to take her seat. She cried out, Noooooo! and she suddenly woke up. It was a dream. Jesus! thank you.

As she was still thinking about the scary dream, the doorbell rang. Griiiiiiiiin! Michelle ran to the door to check who was at the door. Eek Flora! Welcome to my house. It's my pleasure flora replied. Flora was Michelle,s colleague in school. The bond of their friendship is so tight that both often visit each other. Michelle was a pastor's daughter, and she was the only daughter of Pastor and Mrs. John.

She was born again as to the belief of the Christians, to fulfill the scriptures (John3:3-6)

"Jesus answered and said to him, most assuredly, I say to you, unless one is born again, he cannot see the kingdom of God. Nicodemus said to Him, how can a man be born when he is old? Can he enter a second time into his mother's womb and be born?"

Jesus answered, most assuredly, I say to you, unless one is born of water and the Spirit, he cannot enter the kingdom of God. That which is born of the flesh is flesh, and that which is born of the Spirit is spirit. John 3:3-6: NKJV)." This scripture was the beginning of michelle's growth into the realm of the supernatural. Believing what Jesus Christ did on the cross of Calvary spurred her up.

Being a child of the most-high God, she was filled with the knowledge of God and was enthusiastic to do the things of God. Her growth in supernatural reality – spiritual capability and sensitivity was increasing daily. She was the coordinator of the spinster's forum – *Noble Bride*, in her father's church. Aside from being respected as General Overseer's daughter, her geometric spiritual maturity cannot be overlooked. She is a frontrunner of an honest example.

Often, she affirms that *"My parent made the way, but I made a choice. I am not like this because my parents choose. I decided to serve God, and I wasn't forced into the folds. It was my personal decision, that's why I am comfortable, and I don't*

have to struggle with it. "this was her confession, to hold firmly

to what she believes.

Chapter 2

An Invite

Flora came purposely to invite Michelle to a program in her course mate's church. Michelle has been longing to see one of her favorite gospel singers – *Peter Paul*. Michelle asked, what kind of program are you inviting me for? Flora replied, it's a praise vigil, and the guest artist is Peter Paul. When she heard about the guest artist, she became overwhelmed with joy, what!!! Serious??? I will be fully present for the program, Michelle replied. She was so happy because it will be a privilege she has been waiting to experience and this will be an opportunity for her to see Peter Paul – her favorite Artist. It will be a great privilege to meet that man of God.

Flora had a pleasant time with Michelle as they played, discussed a lot of things afterward, and also shared the word of God.

♦ ♦ ♦

Later that evening

Michelle walked up to her dad to ask for his permission to attend the program which was to hold on the 15th of that month.

Dad, Michelle called.

Yes princess, pastor John answered while flipping through his bible how are you today? I'm good Dad, she replied. Dad, I need your permission. Flora and I were invited for a program. She continues her request as she sat beside her dad. It's an all-night program and PETER PAUL will be there live.

Woooooow, amazing, her dad exclaimed, when will this be? so that I may also prepare to attend, her Dad responded. That was just a teased though.

15th of this month he asked? And Michelle replied yes dad. You have my permission, but make sure you inform your mum, said her dad.

Michelle jumped for joy, appreciating her Dad for the privilege given to her to attend the program.

◆ ◆ ◆

On the fifteenth

The day of the praise night finally came, and Michelle had finished up her house chores as quick as possible. Here comes the evening, Flora came and they both left for the program. Flora's course mate – Janet was one of the member of the church. Janet crossed their path after receiving a phone call from Flora, that she was already at the venue. Oh! I am with just two tickets Janet said, being surprised seeing michelle beside Flora.

Flora, why did you bring her with you please? Janet asked.

Oh, friend, I'm so sorry, meet Michelle – my best friend and also my pastor's only daughter, she introduced. Wow, nice! You ought to have told me about her coming before now, so I could get an additional ticket, I have just two reservations, Janet said.

That's fine, Michelle said. I will be comfortable anywhere in the auditorium. What matters is our sincere worship in God's presence.

◆ ◆ ◆

At the venue

Michelle entered and felt goosebumps all over her. This is a large church she thought in her heart. But in a glance, she started having some awkward feelings about her presence in the program.

Oh Lord, I hope I'm In the Right Place, *she thought in her heart.* I don't feel comfortable. She was still muttering when Flora called, Michy, are you ok?

I'm not, Michelle replied. I'm not just feeling comfortable.

Janet was looking at her with so much despite, and with resentment that she said this place is the house of God, friend! why being uncomfortable?

Michelle exhaled. I can feel a heavy presence of marine demons in this place, she replied to her.

Janet got angry; will you stop these unpleasant thoughts. This is a house of God, don't disparage my church, Janet responded.

Flora said; Janet, don't be angry ; Michelle is spiritually gifted. She may sense the presence of some spirits who have the aim to disrupt the program.

Hmm, there is more to this HOLY GHOST, Michelle replied. Janet hissed and went inside the auditorium.

Michelle looked at her wristwatch; it was just 9:45 pm. Its already late she muttered;

◆ ◆ ◆

The program started

The program started, and Michelle wasn't comfortable at all. As Praise session continues, she was uncomfortable. The presence of marine spirit was evident to her. People were busy singing, dancing and jubilating. She was seated praying. With a glance towards where flora was sitting, she realized Flora had been overwhelmed with the praise session and was dancing. Some minutes after the praise session, it was announced that Peter Paul could not make it to the program. Everyone felt disappointed including Michelle. Because the reason she was there in the first place was to meet peter paul.

Chapter 3
Darkness Uncovered

Here comes the time for the main message. A woman was invited to the podium as ***Queen Jezreel***. As she collected the microphone, Michelle's eyes was opened, and she saw that the person with the mic was a golden fish with a long tail.

Blood of Jesus Christ she muttered. Queen Jezreel looked straight at her and called, young lady!

Michelle answered with shock

-Yes ma,

-Are you ok? replied Queen Jezreel

-yes ma

- Good. Please don't be distracted. Just listen to the word of God.

Queen Jezreel continued her message. As she continues, Michelle saw another vision. She saw that the altar was a big ocean with millions of mermaids. And immediate she saw this, she muttered strongly;

Blood of Jesus Christ. Holy ghost!!! What place is this? What have I gotten myself into? Oh Jesus, save me please, she repeatedly muttered.

The woman turned to Michelle again. Michelle could sense the fury in her eyes.

Arrrgh, I did not even pray before I took a step of attending the program, I was so carried away by the guest – Peter Paul and didn't know it was just a scam to gather people. Michelle looked around the auditorium. Jesus! Come and rescue me today, I promise to be careful next time.

And again, she looked at where Flora was seating; she was busy enjoying the sermon and shouting amen to queen Jezreel's declarations. Michelle shook her head. If only she knew or could see what I just saw, she thought in her heart.

Soon the message was over, and the minister gave some announcements.

-Somebody shouted glory when I was preaching, and God laid in my heart to help those people sitting on the white chairs. Please wait behind to see me.

The auditorium has three colors of chairs arranged in it – blue, yellow, and white. Those sitting on the white chairs saw it as a privilege to see queen Jezreel.

Queen Jezreel pointed at Michelle.

- You! young lady (she sneered pointing at Michelle) daughter of the most-high. Hey!!!! I see so much anointing on you. Step out; the Lord said I should lay my hands on you.

 Michelle stood up but refused to step out.

Queen Jezreel smiled and said, God told me you will refuse, and he told me to help you. Wait and see me before you leave.

Michelle replied by saying, don't bother ma. Thanks so much.

Hahahahaha Queen Jezreel laughed. The Lord told me you will be stubborn, and you will refuse. You can have your seat, she told michelle.

The program ended at about 4:30 am. Flora was to wait to see the Queen because she was part of the audience that sat on the white chair. While Michelle was waiting, Janet was so mad at her, saying, how dare you? You little brat. How dare you embarrass my pastor? You are such a mug and an ingrate.

Michelle looked straight at her, saying

-You are one of them

 Janet was shocked

- WHAT!!!!

- Yes, you heard me, and the Lord will disgrace you all.

-- hmm, I realize you are full of yourself. Don't dare us, if you still want to live, replied Janet.

---ten thousand of you cannot harm me. I bare on my body the mark of Jesus Christ Michelle responded aggressively.

- Be warned. We are a moving train. Don't stand on our way. We crush without mercy, Janet replied.

- I am a rail. I cannot be crushed, said Michelle.

Just then queen Jezreel, came in between them. Janet!!!

Chapter 4

The Battle Line Drawn

Queen Jezreel emerged. She dragged Janet out.

-What is this argument about? Queen Jezreel asked Janet. You have just ruined my plans by accepting her claims. You should be wise. What is wrong with you? Just a confrontation and you succumbed.

Did I ask you to defend me? I have been haunting her. That lady you see over there – Michelle is sought for by the marine world, and especially by the congregation of the sixth ocean region. Should anything happen, you will pay extremely for it.

-I'm sorry queen. I volunteer myself in this quest, said Janet. Queen Jezreel focused on her and told her; you are not a matched with Michelle.

She is higher than you. I am her only match for now.

- What! Is she that powerful? I am on the 25th marine power region, and you said she is higher than I? Janet exclaimed

- Hmmm, Janet, do you think we are up against a chicken? Go to the control room to examine her profile. Michelle brought down queen Jezebel? replied queen Jezreel

- What! She did that to queen Jezebel?

- Yes, and that is the reason we intended not to destroy her but to be part of us. She was the main reason we organized this program. Listen to me, Janet, do not interfere. Stay clearly off her. She is your superior, said Queen Jezreel.

-Yes, queen. I hail the queen, replied Janet. Then she left.

While Michelle was waiting for flora to come out, she was praying in her spirit, and queen Jezreel walked up to her.

-Anointed one of the most-high, what troubles you? Queen Jezreel asked,

Michelle speaks;

- How dare you drag the name of the Living God in a mud Queen Jezreel, Queen of the 100th marine region? What guts!!!! Be assured that the Lord will expose you. And I, the servant of the highest God, will not rest until you are brought down to nothing.

- I mean no harm. I want to help you. I am Queen Jezreel; this is my Church. I am a minister; she answered her.

- Oh, please, you should know more by now. I recognize your identity. When your superior – Queen Jezebel, came to strike my mum – Mrs. John with sickness, she was crushed by the power in the name of Jesus Christ. Quit the deceit, I know who you are, Michelle replied her.

- Fine. Yes, I am who I am. You need my help; queen Jezreel opened up.

Michelle speaks

- I do not need your help,

My help cometh from the Lord who made heaven and the earth.

He will not suffer my foot to be moved, he who keeps Israel will not slumber, Behold, he who keeps Israel will not slumber nor sleep. The Lord is my keeper, and the Lord is my shield.

Queen Jezreel could not stand the conversation anymore. She was shivering.

- You remain wanted by us. I will frustrate you until you join us. I will cause sadness in your life and bring you much sorrow until you bend to be part of us. Queen Jezreel raged as she speaks.

Michelle replied

- Shadrach, Meshach, and Abednego defeated the fire. Daniel defeated the lion's den. My Lord Jesus Christ defeated the grave. Queen Jezreel, I will defeat you, she stood firmly declaring that before her eyes.

She left, almost immediately flora came out.

- Michelle, who are you talking to? Flora asked

- What kind of question is that? Didn't you see queen Jezreel here? Michelle replied;

- There's nobody here. It is Just you, and besides I have been with queen Jezreel in her office.

- What? Oh, I see. Please let us leave this place. I will explain later; Michelle held flora's right hand and rushed out of the church surrounding. As they continue their journey home, they continue their conversation. What have you been doing there? Michelle asked Flora;

- Counseling o. That woman is indeed a woman of God; Flora replied. She discussed all have been through and decided to help me.

- Did she give you anything to eat? Michelle questioned,

- Yes, Flora replied.

- What!!! And you ate? Michelle exclaimed,

- No oo, she gave me tea, and it was not just me, including everyone who waited. But I didn't take it because it's too early and I haven't brushed.

- Michelle took a deep breath, ha! Thank God. No wonder you still reply sensibly, Michelle replied.

- How do you mean? Flora asked.

- hmm, let's get home first.

- where is Janet?

- she has gone I guess, Flora answered Michelle.

Michelle Advice Flora as they walk side by side home;

Listen, henceforth you must act carefully with Janet. Please.

- Why? Flora asked;

- until we get to our destination, Michelle replied.

They boarded a bus to continue their journey home.

Chapter 5

VISITATION

Michelle entered into her house and had a strange feeling of the presence of an unfamiliar spirit. Immediately she noticed that strange feeling, she started singing;

Power is in your name

Power is in your name

There is Power in the name Jesus Christ

Power is in your name

She walked around the whole building and then went inside her room. She noticed there wasn't anyone at home except for the gateman. The dog kept barking furiously, but she gave less concern about that. As Michelle opened the door of her room, behold she saw queen Jezreel seated on the cushion in her room. Michelle got furious.

- How dare you? What gut!!! Are you not afraid? What are you doing in my room? Don't you know that light and darkness are two parallel lines that can never meet?

- Michelle, I mean no harm. Again, you delivered one of our captives, Queen Jezreel said.

- Point of correction demon!!!, I did not deliver her. My Father – the Lord God Almighty did. That subtility won't work with me. You won't inject pride in my spirit, Michelle exclaimed.

- (Jezreel stood up) why are you rigid? Loosen up. Listen to me; you need our help. Don't you want to be famous? You have powers, and people need you, you have been given supernatural abilities of a seer, the world will crawl to your doorstep for solutions.

Dear Michelle, we will make you famous and wealthy that governors, kings, dignitaries will flock around you. You will still use the name of the Lord. you will always tell people to turn from their iniquities. We want you to join us. The marine is so much interested in your family; Queen Jezreel implores Michelle.

- Shut up, demon!!! Michelle replied to her.

- don't call me the devil; I am a queen, said Queen Jezreel

- Demon, that's what you are. And all power has been bestowed upon me by my Lord Jesus Christ. He has given me the keys of the kingdom (Michelle started speaking in tongues) that what so ever I bind here on earth, is restricted in heaven and what so ever I loose here on earth is loosed in heaven.

Jezreel, I release in this room the flood of fire from above, Michelle aggressive spoke out.

- Stop it Jezreel shouted,

-Fire! Fire!! Fire!!!!

-arrrrrrrrrrrrghhhhhhh, Michelle, I will deal with you for this. You will suffer for this, and I will make sure the anguish start now in your life and family. I am Queen Jezreel, the golden fish of the 100th marine province, I will deal treacherously with you.

Michelle speaks- you can never touch me because I am the anointed of the highest God, no weapon, formed against me shall prosper, and every tongue that rises against me shall be condemned. Now demon, in the name of *Jesus Christ Of Nazareth, GET OUT*

Chapter 6
Tragedy Strikes

◆ ◆ ◆

The battle began

Just then, her mother opened the door. Michelle was sweating. The dog stopped barking.

-Michy, is there a problem?

- Mum, the queen of the marine coast, that you saw in your revelation was here.

- ***Blood of Jesus Christ, What***! In this house? Her mum exclaimed.

- I brought this upon us. I carnally went to that church program. Lord, I ask for mercy (Michelle cries).

No no, no dear, don't say that. We were all spiritually careless. Michelle's mum – Roselline said God had shown mercy unto us by giving you victory.

As they continue their discussion, Jimmy – the gatekeeper rushed in

-Madam!! Madam!!! Accident !!!Accident!!!

-What, where? Jesus!!!

Michelle and her mum rushed out. Behold Nickson - Michelle's only brother and Pastor John's only son in the pool of his blood, hit by a vehicle as he tried to cross the main road to get into the house.

He was immediately rushed to the hospital for proper care

♦ ♦ ♦

At the hospital

Nickson became unconscious because he fell with his head. He had a big tear at the back of his head, and he was instantly moved to the *Intensive Care Unit* (ICU), for an operation.

Pastor (Mrs) John could not be comforted. Michelle was crying. Pastor John wasn't left out of the sad actions. He pleaded with the doctor to do everything possible to save his only son.

After a week, Nickson was still unconscious. Michelle stayed by his side all through, praying in different ways that she knows. She prayed and prayed and prayed!!!

One night, her parents were at the church for their monthly vigil program. Michelle was alone sleeping after so many prayers.

◆ ◆ ◆

Michelle Tempted

Queen Jezreel came into the room.

-Well, what do we have here?

- What are you doing here, demon? Michelle replied angrily.

- I told you, you will need my help. You have been praying for a week now, and there have not been changes. Would you want your only brother and your father's only son to die? Queen Jezreel requested

Michelle! Say yes, join us, and your brother will be fine, queen Jezreel persuaded her.

Michelle speaks

- Listen to me Jezreel; I serve a God who gives life. And that God is your creator too, he gave me dominion over you. Read my lips demon; I will not sell my soul to you; my whole being belongs to God.

- Queen Jezreel reacted angrily saying since you refuse, prepare to bury your brother.

Michelle replied quoting the scripture

- That's a lie. Who is he that speaks, and it comes to pass when the Lord has not spoken? His life is hidden in Christ and Christ in God. Jezreel, give up the chase. I serve the Lord, and he will deliver me from the snare of the fowler and their noisome pestilence.

For surely they shall gather, but not by him, whosoever shall gather, shall fall for my sake. No weapon, fashioned against

Nickson shall prosper, and every tongue that riseth in judgment shall be condemned. It is my heritage as a child of God. Jezreel, you can do nothing. The God of Daniel will deliver me from your plans.

- Stubborn fellow. We shall see, Queen Jezreel replied Michelle.

Michelle started praying again. All through that night, she could not sleep.

◆ ◆ ◆

Turmoil

In the morning, a nurse came to inject Nickson. She placed another infusion and injected it into Nickson's body and left.

Few minutes later, Nickson started convulsing. Just then, Pastor and his wife arrived and met Michelle shouting and crying. What happen, they both exclaimed, when pastor's wife – who was Michelle's mum saw her son's condition, she fainted.

The nurse had mistakenly administered the wrong injection. Hell was let loose. Pastor John wasn't seeing it funny. He threatened to arrest the nurse. Some elders and church members had followed them to check on nickson. The hospital became a centre of hot arguments like a shout like rain of fire and brimstone. The atmosphere was tensed with chaos as some of the members wasn't taking the matter cheap.

Only Michelle understood what was going on. Amidst her pain, she took it upon herself to talk to them saying;
-Brethren, this is not time to sue anybody. It is time to war with prayers. The devil according to God's word, walks about like a roaring lion seeking whom to devour. It is time to pray.
As she spoke, Pastor John noticed that Nickson – his son has stopped breathing.

The doctor walked into the ward and examined his pulse and shook his head. He reached out for the bed cloth and covered him.

- We lost him, Pastor.

Pastor screamed. He just lost his only son.

- Jesus! No, Jesus, you can't fail me. My only son can't die.

Members and elders present could not hold back their tears. They helped to console Pastor John.

Michelle stood by her brother. Tears rolled down her face. She shouted,

-Nooo, Jesus nooo. Nickson is not dead. (crying) *since I was born, and now I'm getting old, I have never seen the righteous forsaken or the children of the living God beg for bread.*

(She ran outside and went on her knees facing the sun.)

- oh Lord, God of heaven, remember. (Crying) my father and my God, remember how my parents have walked before you, in truth and with a perfect heart.

Remember now, oh Lord, my service in your kingdom. Remember now, oh Lord, your promises to my family. You said you will not suffer your holy one to see corruption. Oh Lord God (crying) shall the dead praise you? Nickson is the pianist in your church, oh Lord how then can he play to you those sweet melodies that arouse the magnitude of your greatness.

Heavenly father, they that trust in you shall be like mount Zion that cannot be moved but abides forever.

(She opened her eyes and turned around, here she saw Queen Jezreel standing before her.

- for the last time Michelle, accept my proposal and your brother will live.

Michelle replied to her;

- You demon from the pit of hell. If my God won't save me, then so be it. As for me and my house, we will serve the living God. *My hope is built on nothing else but Jesus blood and righteousness, I dare not trust the vainest thing but wholly lean on Jesus name.*

On Christ, the solid rock I stand. All other grounds is sinking sand. My faith looks up to him my lamb of Calvary, Savior divine.

He will not suffer my foot to be moved. He who keeps me will not slumber. He will fight for me, and I will hold my peace.

(Speaking in tongues)

She began to worship.

The lord that does wonders

You are the God of remarkable wonders

I've tasted of your power

The lord that does wonders

You have shown me so much mercy. Much more than I deserves.

The words you speak

Turns things around

Your outstretched arm has lifted me

You took away, the chains and colts

That held me bound.

(Speaking in tongues)

You are mighty

As she worshipped, everyone worshipped with her. They were all

outside when the unusual happened.

Nickson walked out of the ward by himself, Nickson!!! Pastor
John exclaimed, with a rush he went straight to hug him.
Praise ye the lord

He is a man of war.

They all praised the name of the lord. It was a double celebration.

Pastor Mrs. John Roseline was revived, and Nickson came back

to life. Everyone were amazed with what happen and some of

them couldn't stop adoring the sovereign God. Meanwhile the

next day was a Sunday. They all left praising God.

Great thanksgiving was held in God's household – church. The

Members of the church appreciated God with songs of praise and

worship was rendered unto God when they heard about the
testimonies. It was indeed an excellent service.

Chapter 7
The Rape

On Sunday night, at about 8: 55 p.m, the family of pastor John were all seated in the Living room when they heard the doorbell rang. Usually, Jimmy – the gateman calls with the inter-com to inform the family about any visitor that comes. But that night, that wan,t the case. There was not pre-information from jimmy.

The doorbell keeps ringing.

Nickson called Jimmy through the intercom, it kept ringing, but he wasn't answering.

Nickson took a step towards the door to see who was at the door. Michelle stopped him.

- Nicky don't! Stay back, Michelle reacted;

- Why? We need to know who's at the door. Maybe Jimmy might have gone to buy something.

- Then we'll wait till we get a call from him, Michelle replied him.

Nickson then sat, but the doorbell won't stop ringing. He picked the phone and called Jimmy again, but he didn't answer.

- It's almost 30minutes. Where could he have gone? Nickson said. I need to go outside and find out.

-Nicky, Michelle called, you are going nowhere.

- Are you serious? Why do you like bossing people around? Nickson reacted,

Pastor John cuts in;

- son, please listen to your sister.

- Yes, nickson, said Roseline. She said don't go out, please, listen to her and don't go out.

- This is really unfair mum, replied Nickson. It is always about what Michelle sees and says. I am her elder brother. She should stop giving commands.

- Nickson, this not about bossing you around, I am only following God's instruction. We must not open the door no matter what, Michelle replied.

Nickson called Jimmy again, but he wasn't answering. He tried his mobile line, but it was switched off. The bell rang once again, and Nickson moved to open the door. Michelle tried stopping him, but she could not overpower him, he eventually opened the door and saw three young men standing at the door.

The three men were on suits; they greeted Nicky. The first man asked about his dad – who was a pastor. They have come to congratulate him for what God did in their family.

- Oh, that's good, but it's late. You can't see the pastor now. Please, tomorrow morning should be proper because he won't be able to attend to anyone.

- We are travelling tonight; we won't make it to seeing him tomorrow, the men replied him.

- I see. Please wait here, let me inform him, Nickson replied.

As Nickson tried going in, the men forced themselves in and brought out guns and shot him on the leg.

---Oh God my leg, Nickson shouted

- Shut- up! One of the men shouted. Pastor, I heard you collected a lot of money today. Bring it out!!!

He sighted Michelle.

- Woah, you have a beautiful daughter, baby, put yourself together.

- For what? Replied Michelle. Don't dare come close to me.

The man slapped Michelle. He wants to rape her.

- My friend arranges yourself.

- I know you love your father; I will shoot your dad and mum if you do not arrange yourself after the count of ten. - I rather die than allow you to touch mum, Michelle replied.

- Don't bother counting, because I will not. Please leave my parents and go ahead and shoot me, Michelle replied to him

- 1, 2,3,4,5, 6.....…......

- Michelle! Do as they said. Don't let dad and mom die, please. Nickson pleaded still bleeding from the shot. (Crying)

Pastor and his wife started pleading with Michelle. The man was still counting.

7, 8, 9, ...

Immediately he stopped the count, he dropped his gun and forcefully carried Michelle. She was raped until she went unconscious — they left her and left in a hurry, leaving the family in a thick sadness.

Mummy shouted, help! Help! Help! Nickson was crawling towards where Michelle was, and Pastor Held her tight wailing, Michelle's Mum – Roseline crying out for help. Jimmy – the gateman was locked by the three men inside his toilet.

Pastor John and his wife carried both Michelle and Nickson to the car, and they were quickly rushed to the hospital.

Disobedience Opens Door for Disaster.

Chapter 8

Coma

Nickson and Michelle were placed in different wards, and treatment began with immediate effect as they got to the hospital. Roseline – Michelle's Mum wasn't settled in her mind; she kept walking from one place to another in the hospital. Pastor John picked his phone to call one of his Elders – Elder James, to inform him what had happened again. The Elder immediately called the leader of the prayer intercessor Brother Ronald, and they all rushed, including his wife to the hospital to see pastor John's Family.

The bullet was soon removed, and the leg was treated. Nickson won't stop shouting;

I need to see my sister – Michelle, he meant.

I caused this tragedy upon her.

I was stubborn.

I disobeyed her because I felt I was the elder..

I had a wrong feeling, and I felt she was bossing me around.

If I had obeyed, this wouldn't have happened to her. She wouldn't have been raped.

As at that time, Jimmy – The gateman had been unlocked from the toilet by Roseline when she ran out for help before they rushed to the hospital.

Elder James, his wife and the leader of the prayer intercessor arrived at the hospital, and they saw pastor John crying saying;

Oh Lord, what have I done to deserve this?

I gave my whole heart to you.

I served you with all my heart, all my soul and all my strength according to your word.

I kept to your commandment by training my children in the way of the Lord.

I gave myself always to obey you and walk according to your will.

Father, why will my only daughter be raped. She has always been committed to your work and your will.

Michelle! Come back, come back, come back! He cries out in front of the hospital's building.

Elder James approached and comforted him while his wife went to comfort pastor John's wife.

Pastor, do not worry; Elder James said

The Lord is with us like a mighty warrior, so our persecutor will stumble and not prevail, they will fail and be thoroughly disgraced; their dishonor will never be forgotten.

Brother Ronald went to a corner at the hospital and started praying in tongues for the Lord to intervene.

It was already 2:05 a:m, on Monday morning. Everywhere was cold, Brother Ronald was still praying, Nickson's leg had been stitched, he was given a pain relief pills, and he was fast asleep. Pastor Mrs. John was lying down helplessly groaning as Elder

James' wife continue to pet her. She continues to comfort her using several scriptures. Elder James was right beside Pastor John; they both held each other hands praying.

Soon Dr. Albert saunters into his office, and as he was sighted by Pastor John, he ran to him to ask about the well being of his children. The Doctor invited him to his office, while Elder James and pastor John went straight to Dr Albert office to hear the latest update about the well being of his children.

Dr. Albert speaks;

Pastor, I'm sorry for what happened, Nickson had been attended to, presently he is fast asleep. The bullet has been removed, and the wound was stitched. He was later given pain relief drugs so that he can be relieved and have a good sleep.

But for Michelle; he sighed.

What happened!!! Pastor John exclaimed;

Calm down sir, the doctor replied;

She is still in a coma; let us keep praying. I believe she will regain consciousness soon. Pastor John focused his eyes on the doctor as tears drop from his eyes. Elder James couldn't hold it but instead told the Doctor to keep close eyes on Michelle, and they must not stop treatment. He additionally promised to foot all the hospital bills. Elder James held Pastor John's hand as they both leave the doctor's office.

Immediately Roseline – Michelle's mum saw her husband. She ran to him, saying, Dear, what happened? Is Michelle dead? Tell me she is gone, so I will know the Lord hasn't done it well. Elder James' wife held her and took her to where she was sitting. Elder James responded to her saying, Michelle is not dead, but the doctor said, she is still in Coma, and they should continue praying that she may regain consciousness as fast as possible.

◆ ◆ ◆

Michelle in the marine world

Michelle's body was left on the bed, and artificial oxygen was passed and connected to her nose to sustain her while she lay down helplessly in a coma.

Michelle's spirit left her. She finds herself in a deserted place – she was in a revelation. Her spirit is entirely in another place. She found herself on an island.

What am I doing here? She asked herself.

She cries out, is anybody here?

Mummy, where are you?

Daddy, where are you?

Nickson, please come out, where are you?

She keeps wandering alone until she gets to a point, where she could only see a big ocean before her. Nowhere to go, where will I go? Where!

Immediately, she halted and looked up to the sky, crying oh God, rescue me from this obscurity! At that moment, she remembers one of David writings in the book of psalms, (Psalm 139).

She looks up again to the sky and cries out;

Oh lord,

You have searched me, LORD,

  and you know me.

You know when I sit and when I rise;

  you perceive my thoughts from afar.

You discern my going out and my lying down;

  you are familiar with all my ways.

Before a word is on my tongue

  you, LORD, know it ultimately.

You hem me in behind and before,

  and you lay your hand upon me.

Such knowledge is too wonderful for me,

  too lofty for me to attain.

Where can I go from your Spirit?

  Where can I flee from your presence?

If I go up to the heavens, you are there;

if I make my bed in the depths, you are there.

If I rise on the wings of the dawn,

if I settle on the far side of the sea,

even there your hand will guide me,

your right hand will hold me fast.

If I say, "Surely the darkness will hide me

and the light become night around me,"

even the darkness will not be dark to you;

the night will shine like the day,

for darkness is as light to you.

For you created my inmost being;

you knit me together in my mother's womb. (Psalm 139) NIV.

Oh Lord, I don't know where I am. I know there is no place your eyes do not reach, please my father rescue me from this deserted land.

As she readjusted her head, she saw **Queen Jezreel.**

Haaahaaaahaaaahaaa, Queen Jezreel laughed, I came to offer you what you will forever be grateful, but you rejected my offer. The marine world wants you; they need you, and they are ready to give you anything you want, but you refuse the offer. Who can rescue you now? Call on anybody, no one will hear you. This is our territory, and no one can deliver you. This is your last chance. You are in between life and death. You are in a coma. We can decide to kill you, and you won't be restored to life, and we can decide to restore you to life. All you need to do, to live again is to accept our offer; *Queen Jezreel* said, and laughed; hahaha.

She held Michelle and pushed her into the sea.

Chapter 9

The Real Battle

It is already 7:00 a:m, on Monday morning. Brother Ronald was fast asleep, pastor John was fast asleep, Elder James was beside pastor John fast asleep, and both pastor John's wife and Elder James' wife was also sleeping. Brother Ronald stood up. Eek, it's 7:00a:m. He went directly to where the pastor and Elder were to wake them up. As at that time, Nickson was already awake, and they all went to see how he was doing.

Nickson speaks;

Mum, he started crying, where is Michelle? He asked; the mum was about to burst into tears when Pastor John reacted. Enough of all these tears, Michelle is fine. We need to continue praying for her. She needs our prayer.

Go and prepare food for Nickson so that he can eat, pastor John said. Brother Ronald informed the pastor that he would call for an intercessory meeting, and they would start prayers as soon as they meet. We will pray until Michelle regains her consciousness. Elder James' wife informed her husband to call the housemaid to prepare their children for school, that they will not be coming back home soon. She decides to help Roseline – Michelle's mum with all she needs to do and to keep encouraging her. Elder James chose to stay close with the pastor.

Elder James contacted the other ministers to continue running the weekly church activities. Everyone left for what they were supposed to do, while Elder James and Pastor John stayed with Nickson in the hospital. Nickson lay down on the bed, to pray to God on her sister behalf. Pastor John and Elder James were walking around the whole room, praying for Michelle. Mr Ronald called some of his available prayer intercessors, and they started praying for Michelle. The atmosphere was becoming tense with the incense of prayer for Michelle.

◆ ◆ ◆

Michelle amid Marine spirit.

Queen Jezreel pushed Michelle, and they both find themselves in the deep – amidst the marine ghosts, mermaids, marine agents, and Queen Bezel – the number 1 queen of the Marine spirit. They have chosen that day for a meeting, to bring Michelle into their midst, and not only to bring her into their midst but to also initiate her as the Number 2 Queen of the Marine spirit.

The three men that came to Pastor John's house were sent by Queen Jezreel, to harm the whole family and put them into a state of turmoil. They plan to make sure Michelle was brought to that meeting – marine annual world meeting. Michelle unconsciousness wasn't a coincidence; it was all planned. They all sat in levels as their rank was, while Queen Bezel sits in the highest seat as the leader of the marine agents.

Michelle stood boldly before them, while they spoke to her at first, to join them.

Queen Jezreel spoke,

She has been adamant and stubborn. It took me a lot of time and stress to bring her down here. Now that she is here, we can initiate her to occupy her position. Michelle sighted Janet; she was among the second rank Marine spirits. I wasn't surprised, right from the day I met her; I knew she was part of them.

Queen Bezel speaks;

Michelle, I have been monitoring you, right from the day you were born. Your Parents have been the one protecting us from getting you. You were trained up in the way of that your God. While you were in primary school, we sent one of our agents to apply for a teaching job in your school, of which she was successfully employed. Michelle! Do you remember, Miss Rita? When you were in Nursery class, Miss Rita was sent to initiate you by giving you candies, but there was no time she gave you goodies, that you didn't take it home. But your mum will neither allow you to collect things from outsiders nor eat it without their consent.

During your primary levels, we sent another marine agent to you as a friend, do you remember Lizzy? She was your closest friend, but you never for once collect anything to eat from her. This was because your parent trained you up, not to ever collect things from outsiders. All through your days in secondary school, we tried different ways, including sending a guys to you, that you may lust after them, and fall outside God's grace. But instead you were growing stronger in the Lord, and your parents helped you build your prayer life by allowing you go for three days fasting and prayer (marathon) every last three days of the months. This alone made us re-strategize on how we can initiate you. That was why we struck your mum with an attack, but she was rescued.

The program was organized basically because of you. We knew you like Peter Paul, and the only way we can get your attention and lure you into our midst is to organized the program, but you eventually didn't fall into the trap.

Now this is the last chance for you, it is either you join us or die, Queen Bezel shouted. You have wasted a lot of my time getting you little brat.

Michelle laughed aloud; hahaha

Which life do you want to take? My life? Michelle asked as she looks at all the marine agents. She looks straight to queen Bezel and said; no one can take my life, for I am dead, and my life is hidden in Christ. If you need to take my life, you will have to take the life of Christ first.

Queen Bezel stood up, she shouted, she was angry. You dare not talk to me like that. You dare not experience what I can do!!!

Who are you? Michelle replied, for he who lives in me is greater than he who lives in the world, including all of you.

Queen Bezel said, you are ready to die forever, then everywhere began to shake. Meanwhile, it was already midnight (Tuesday morning). Mr. Ronald and the other prayer colleagues were in the church praying to God on behalf of Michelle, that she may regain consciousness. Elder James and Pastor John were in Nickson's ward praying also. Pastor Mrs Roselin John and Elder James' wife were in Pastor John's house in warfare prayer.

The Battle became tough as all the marine Agents gather up to launch an attack on Michelle, that her soul may perish, and that she may not be able to come back to life.

Then Michelle rage quoting the scriptures,

Whoever dwells in the shelter of the Most-High

will rest in the shadow of the Almighty.

I will say of the LORD, "He is my refuge and my fortress,

my God, in whom I trust."

Surely he will save me

from the fowler's snare

and from the deadly pestilence.

He will cover me with his feathers,

and under his wings, I will find refuge;

his faithfulness will be my shield and rampart.

I will not fear the terror of night,

nor the arrow that flies by day,

nor the pestilence that stalks in the darkness,

nor the plague that destroys at midday.

A thousand may fall at my side,

ten thousand at my right hand,

but it will not come near me.

I will only observe with my eyes

and see the punishment of the wicked.

For I know, "The LORD is my refuge,"

and I make the Most-High my dwelling,

no harm will overtake me;

no disaster will come near my tent.

For he will command his angels concerning me

to guard me in all your ways;

As she quotes that verse, Michelle's eyes were open and she saw

an uncountable chariot of angels around her, and she continues;

they will lift me in their hands

   so that I will not strike my foot against a stone.

I will tread on the lion and the cobra;

   I will trample the great lion and the serpent.

"Because he loves me," says the LORD, "I will rescue him;

   I will protect him, for he acknowledges my name.

I will call on him, and he will answer me;

   he will be with me in trouble;

 He will deliver me and honor me.

With long life He will satisfy me

   and show me my salvation."

The marine agents gather together as Queen Bezel leads to send the most dreadful hurricane-force to destroy Michelle. They don't use this power except for the most powerful creature that has equivalent power with their Number 1 Queen.

Michelle shouted;

They shall come in flood, but my God shall raise a standard against them.

In the name of Jeeeesusss Christ,

As she mentioned that name, she stretches out her hands towards the hurricane-force that was sent by queen Bezel and her agents, and there came from her direction, a powerful eruption that has never happened in the history of the world, it swallows up both the hurricane force and the whole agents of Marine world including Queen Bezel. Suddenly the entire place was empty and calm, and a mighty hand drew her out of the waters. And immediately she panted up on the hospital bed and woke up exactly 5:00a:m on Tuesday Morning.

And a nurse saw her and ran to the doctor's office, doctor! Doctor! Doctor! She exclaimed. The lady in ward 301 is awake. The Doctor ran immediately to the department and found Michelle sitting on the Bed. He was amazed and couldn't explain what had happened. Michy! How are you feeling? I am entirely okay Michelle replied, and started singing;

thank you thank you, Lord

thank you, Lord,

thank you, Lord, for everything you have done.

Pastor John and Elder James walked in as they overheard the Nurse as she was talking to the doctor about the lady in ward 301. Pastor John hugs her daughter, and she narrated all that happened while she was in Coma to her Dad. And they dance and celebrate. Pastor John took his phone to inform his wife that Michelle has regained consciousness, and she was completely fine. Elder James also called Brother Ronald to tell him of the Latest Update. Everybody rushed down to the hospital to see Michelle. Nickson woke up and was helped to Michelle's room. He pleaded, but Michy told him, everything worked together for good for them, and also said it was the Lord's doing and it was marvelous in their sight.

Everyone came, and they all glorified God for winning the battle. They all rejoice. After two days, both Nickson and Michelle were discharged, and they happily went back home.

I believe you learnt something tangible in this storyline. The best you can do to help yourself overcome the world is to equip your self with the power of the Holyspirit. Don't forget what *Ephesian 6:12 says;*

" *We do not wrestle against flesh and blood, but against principalities, power, the rulers of the darkness of this age, spiritual hosts of wickedness in the heavenly places"*

The devil keeps roaming around finding people he wants to devour, and destroy. He comes but to steal, kill, and destroy (John 10:10).

It is not too late to start equipping yourself. Someone may be out there haunting you without your awareness. Michelle was haunted from the day she was birthed. Be vigilant, watchful, and prayerful.

Be sensitive to ***Dark Aura.***

About the Author

Adegboye Samuel is a great writer. He has been writing since he was in high school. While studying he has written a lot of articles that have blessed lives; his storyline ranges from Fictions to Christian piece of literature, fairy tales and poet. He also has educational publication like books and video tutorials. He is a lover of God and believers.

Acknowledgements

First of all, my appreciation goes to God, Almighty for the opportunity to collate this manuscript. I am grateful to number of friends, colleagues, and co-members in encouraging and supporting me to start the work, persevere with it, and finally to publish it.

THANKS FOR READING

www.ingramcontent.com/pod-product-compliance
Lightning Source LLC
Chambersburg PA
CBHW051237120626
46547CB00013B/1678